Learn to Draw
Military Vehicles

www.av2books.com

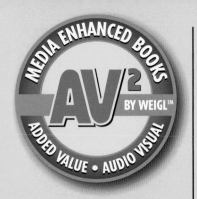

AV² provides enriched content that supplements and complements this book. Weigl's AV² books strive to create inspired learning and engage young minds in a total learning experience.

Your AV² Media Enhanced books come alive with...

Audio
Listen to sections of the book read aloud.

Key Words
Study vocabulary, and complete a matching word activity.

Video
Watch informative video clips.

Quizzes
Test your knowledge.

Embedded Weblinks
Gain additional information for research.

Slide Show
View images and captions, and prepare a presentation.

Try This!
Complete activities and hands-on experiments.

... and much, much more!

Go to **www.av2books.com**, and enter this book's unique code.

BOOK CODE

J145818

AV² by Weigl brings you media enhanced books that support active learning.

Published by AV² by Weigl
350 5th Avenue, 59th Floor
New York, NY 10118
Website: www.weigl.com   www.av2books.com

Library of Congress Cataloging-in-Publication Data

Military vehicles / [edited by] Heather Kissock.
     pages cm -- (Learn to draw)
ISBN 978-1-61913-242-9 (hardcover : alk. paper) -- ISBN 978-1-61913-247-4
(softcover : alk. paper)
1. Vehicles, Military, in art--Juvenile literature. 2.
Drawing--Technique--Juvenile literature. I. Kissock, Heather.
NC825.M54M55 2012
743'.8962374--dc23
                          2012000466

Printed in the United States of America in North Mankato, Minnesota
1 2 3 4 5 6 7 8 9 0 16 15 14 13 12

042012
WEP050412

Senior Editor: Heather Kissock
Art Director: Terry Paulhus

Every reasonable effort has been made to trace ownership and to obtain permission to reprint copyright material. The publishers would be pleased to have any errors or omissions brought to their attention so that they may be corrected in subsequent printings.

Weigl acknowledges Getty Images as its primary image supplier for this title.

Contents

Why Draw?

Drawing is easier than you think. Look around you. The world is made of shapes and lines. By combining simple shapes and lines, anything can be drawn. An orange is just a circle with a few details added. A flower can be a circle with ovals drawn around it. An ice cream cone can be a triangle topped with a circle. Almost anything, no matter how complicated, can be broken down into simple shapes.

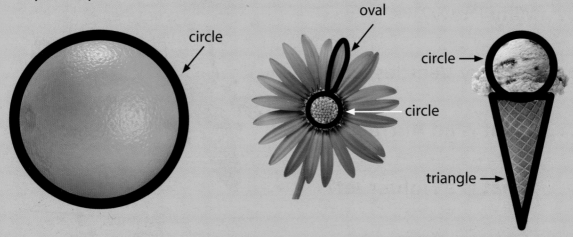

circle

oval

circle

circle

triangle

Drawing helps people make sense of the world. It is a way to reduce an object to its simplest form, say our most personal feelings and thoughts, or show others objects from our **imagination**. Drawing an object can help you learn how it fits together and works.

What shapes do you see in this car?

It is fun to put the world onto a page, but it is also a good way to learn. Learning to draw even simple objects introduces the skills needed to fully express oneself visually. Drawing is an excellent form of **communication** and improves people's imagination.

Practice drawing the military vehicles in this book to learn the basic skills necessary to draw. You can use those skills to create your own drawings.

Military Vehicles

T he main task of the armed forces is to protect their country and its **allies**. A country's armed forces can be made up of several branches. The three main branches are the army, the navy, and the air force. Each division relies on specific equipment to do its job. The equipment has been tailored to protect the country from the ground, the sea, or the air.

Drawing military vehicles is a useful way to learn how the armed forces defend their country. It is also a way to learn how the vehicles protect the soldiers operating them. As you draw the military vehicles in this book, think about what features each vehicle has and how soldiers use the vehicle to stay safe and defend the country.

What is an Aircraft Carrier?

An aircraft carrier is a navy ship that transports jets and other aircraft to where they are needed. Once at the location, the ships serve as home base for the aircraft. The aircraft can take off from the carrier and land on it.

Aircraft carriers are considered to be the lead ship in a **fleet**. Due to their large size, they are one of the most expensive types of ship to build. Only nine countries have aircraft carriers in their armed forces, and most of these countries have no more than two in their fleet.

Flight Deck
The flight deck is the aircraft carrier's runway. Aircraft take off and land on this part of the ship.

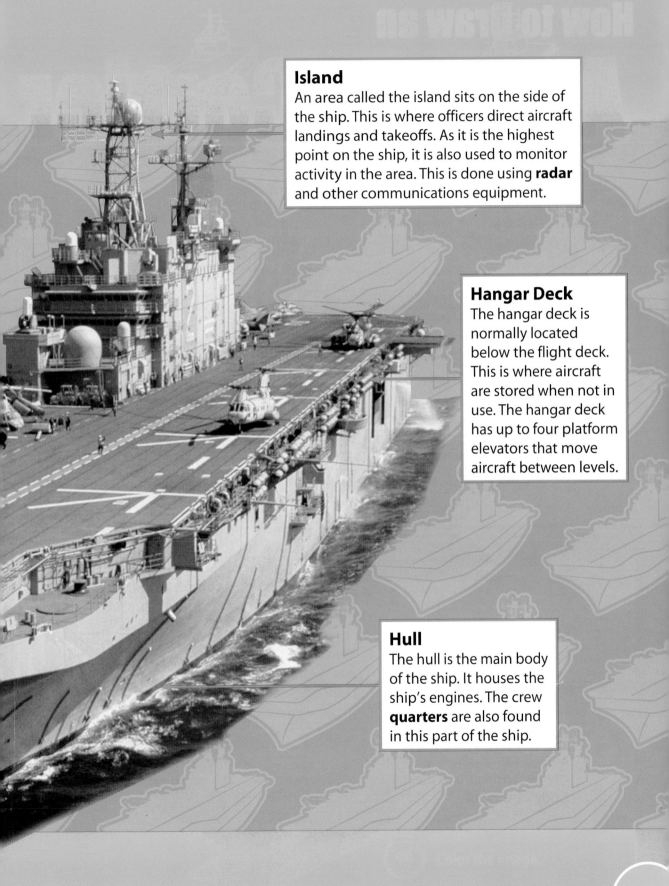

Island
An area called the island sits on the side of the ship. This is where officers direct aircraft landings and takeoffs. As it is the highest point on the ship, it is also used to monitor activity in the area. This is done using **radar** and other communications equipment.

Hangar Deck
The hangar deck is normally located below the flight deck. This is where aircraft are stored when not in use. The hangar deck has up to four platform elevators that move aircraft between levels.

Hull
The hull is the main body of the ship. It houses the ship's engines. The crew **quarters** are also found in this part of the ship.

What is a Fighter Jet?

Fighter jets are made to attack enemies from the sky. They may engage in **combat** with other fighter jets or fire at targets on the ground. Fighter jets are fast and easy to maneuver. This helps them dodge incoming fire.

Fighters have been an important part of the armed forces since World War I. At that time, they were airplanes that were armed with guns. Today, fighters are jet-powered machines, capable of flying beyond the speed of sound.

Cockpit
The pilot sits in the cockpit at the front of the jet. The cockpit contains all of the controls needed to fly the jet and stage attacks.

Radar
A fighter jet's radar system is located on its nose. Radar is used to locate enemies and make maps.

Engines
A fighter jet's engines are at the back of the jet. They provide the **thrust** needed to move the jet forward.

Stabilizers and Rudders
At the rear of the jet are the stabilizers and rudders. The vertical stabilizers help balance the jet. The rudder is used to turn it.

Wings
Like many airplanes, a fighter jet has two wings. The wings generate **lift** so the jet can stay in the air. Each wing has flaps at the back. Flaps can be positioned downward to increase lift. They can also be extended toward the back of the jet to increase **drag**. This will help to slow the jet down during landing.

How to Draw a
Fighter Jet

1 Use an oval and lines to draw a stick figure of the fighter jet, as shown.

2 Draw the wings and missiles.

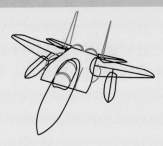

3 Now, draw the cockpit and horizontal stabilizers.

4 Next, add details to the cockpit, and draw the vertical stabilizers and engines.

5 Add details to the missiles and stabilizers.

6 Complete the engines.

7 In this step, add details to the wings and the body of the jet, as shown.

8 Erase the extra lines.

9 Color the image.

What is a Helicopter?

Military helicopters are used to transport soldiers and to conduct **surveillance** missions. They can also be used as combat vehicles. Some military helicopters are small, able to hold only a few people. Others can carry more than 40 people at a time.

Helicopters can do things that most airplanes cannot do. For instance, they are able to hover. This allows people to be lowered to the ground safely. Helicopters also do not need a runway to land or take off. As a result, they can be sent to areas where airplanes cannot go.

Cockpit
The pilot sits in an enclosed cockpit. All of the controls needed to operate the helicopter are found here.

Rotor Blades

A helicopter's rotor blades act as its wings. When the blades begin spinning, air flows over them. This gives the helicopter the lift needed to fly. The position of the blades can be adjusted to lift the helicopter into the air.

Engine

The engine provides the force needed to spin the rotor blades. This force gets the helicopter and its contents into the air.

Landing Skids

Some helicopters sit on their landing skids when they are on the ground. When landing, the skids protect the bottom of the helicopter from damage. Other helicopters sit on wheels.

How to Draw a
Helicopter

1 Draw a stick figure frame of the helicopter. Use ovals and lines to draw the body and rotors.

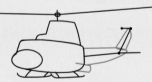

2 Now, draw the rocket launcher and the body of the tail.

3 Next, complete the cockpit, and draw the engine, as shown.

4 Draw the landing skids.

5 In this step, draw the window and add details to the body, as shown.

6 Draw the main rotor and the tail rotor.

7 Add details, as shown.

8 Erase the extra lines.

9 Color the image.

What is a Humvee?

The military uses the humvee mainly to transport soldiers or cargo from one place to another. It was not built as a combat vehicle. It was to be used behind the **front lines**.

In recent years, however, the humvee has been provided with more armor to protect the people inside. Some humvees now have a steel exterior and bullet-resistant glass. Many are also equipped with weapons.

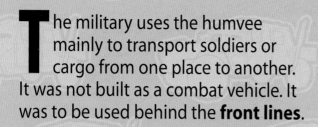

Seating
A humvee can seat up to four people.

4-Wheel Drive
Humvees have 4-wheel drive. This means that the engine powers all four wheels at all times. However, if one of the wheels begins to slip, the engine has the ability to reduce the **torque** on the slipping wheel. This allows the humvee to steady itself.

Size
A humvee is 6 feet (1.8 meters) tall, 7 feet (2.1 m) wide and 15 feet (4.6 m) long. This size makes the vehicle stable on the road.

Fuel
A humvee's gas tank can hold up to 25 gallons (95 liters) of fuel. It can travel 300 miles (480 kilometers) before needing more gas.

Tires
The humvee has tires specially designed for military use. The driver has the ability to reduce the air pressure in the tires while driving. This helps the humvee handle difficult **terrain**.

How to Draw a
Humvee

1 Start with a stick figure frame of the humvee. Draw lines for the body and circles for the tires.

2 Draw the tires.

3 Next, draw the doors of the humvee.

4 Now, draw the windshields, windows, and the front of the vehicle.

5 In this step, draw the lights, iron grill, and exhaust pipe.

6 Add details to the tires.

7 Draw the mirror, wipers, and bolts on the tires, as shown.

8 Erase the extra lines.

9 Color the image.

What is a Submarine?

A submarine is a navy vehicle that can travel underwater. Submarines are fully enclosed. People enter and exit from a **hatch** at the top. When sealed, the hatch makes the submarine completely waterproof.

Submarines are used to search the waters for enemy activity. This can be in the form of other submarines or ships traveling overhead. Submarines are equipped with torpedoes and missiles to handle enemy attack.

Sail

The sail is the prime viewing area for the people inside. Using the **periscope**, the submarine's crew can see what is happening around them. The crew also uses radar and other communications equipment that is located here.

Sonar

Submarines locate objects using sonar. Sonar equipment sends out sound waves. When the waves hit an object, they bounce back to the submarine. The sound lets the submarine crew know where the object is.

Torpedoes

Torpedoes are stored at the front of the submarine. When needed, these weapons are loaded into tubes and fired.

Hull
Some submarines have two hulls. The outer hull is the metal exterior of the vessel. The inner hull protects the people inside from the water pressure found in the deep ocean.

Propeller
The propeller is located at the back end of the submarine. Its spinning action moves the submarine through the water.

Rudder
The rudder rises up from the back of the submarine. It helps steer the submarine from side to side.

Diving Planes
Diving planes come out from the sides of the submarines. They help move the submarine up and down.

How to Draw a
Submarine

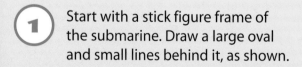

1 Start with a stick figure frame of the submarine. Draw a large oval and small lines behind it, as shown.

2 Draw a base on the top of the submarine.

3 Next, draw the sail.

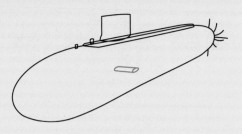

4 Draw the diving plane.

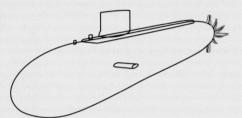

5 In this step, draw the propellers and rudder.

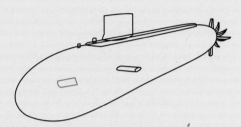

6 Next, draw the torpedo launcher.

7 Add more details to the submarine, as shown.

8 Erase the extra lines.

9 Color the image.

What is a Tank?

The tank is one of the army's main fighting vehicles. It is known for its ability to fire at the enemy while traveling at high speeds over tough terrain. This powerful ground weapon rolls across battlefields, crushing anything that gets in its way.

The first tanks were developed during World War I. Their creation brought an end to the **trench warfare** of the time and moved the fighting aboveground. Today, the tank is considered an essential part of any army.

Turret
The turret sits on top of the hull. It contains the tank's weapons. These may include machine guns, flame throwers, or a cannon. The turret can turn in a full circle. This allows the soldiers inside to aim the weapon in any direction without having to turn the entire vehicle.

Hull
The bottom part of the tank is called the hull. It serves as the body of the tank. The tank's engine is located in the hull. The tracks and wheels are connected to the hull as well.

Hatch

The hatch is located on top of the turret. This is where soldiers get in and out of the tank. During battle, the hatch is normally closed to protect the people inside. To see outside, soldiers use a periscope located in the turret.

Tracks

A tank moves using caterpillar tracks. The tracks fit around the tank's wheels. When the wheels turn, the tracks begin moving as well. Tracks are able to grip the ground better than wheels. The tank can easily move over rough ground as a result.

How to Draw a Tank

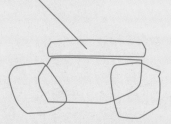

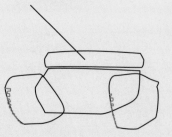

1 First, draw a stick figure frame of the tank. Use lines to draw the body, turret, and tracks.

2 Add details to the tracks.

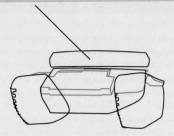
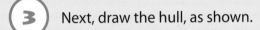

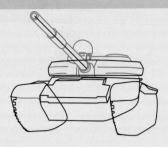

3 Next, draw the hull, as shown.

4 Now, draw the hatch, turret, and main gun.

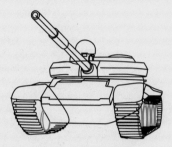

5 Complete the tracks using straight lines.

6 Draw the track wheels.

7 Add details to the vehicle, as shown.

8 Erase the extra lines.

9 Color the image.

Test Your Knowledge of Military Vehicles

1. What is the runway on an aircraft carrier called?

Answer: The flight deck

2. What force pushes a jet forward?

Answer: Thrust

3. What part of a helicopter acts as the vehicle's wings?

Answer: The rotor blades

4. How far can a humvee travel before it needs fuel?

Answer: 300 miles (480 km)

5. Where are a submarine's torpedoes stored?

Answer: At the front of the submarine

6. When were tanks first developed?

Answer: During World War I

Want to learn more? Log on to av2books.com to access more content.

Draw an Environment

Materials
- Large white poster board
- Internet connection or library
- Pencils and crayons or markers
- Glue or tape

Steps
1. Complete one of the military vehicle drawings in this book. Cut out the drawing.
2. Using this book, the internet, or a library, find out about your vehicle and the environment in which it works.
3. Think about the features of this environment. What does it look like? What sorts of objects are found near it? Are there other structures in its environment? What kinds of structures are these? What other important features might you find in this vehicle's environment?
4. On the large white poster board, draw an environment for your vehicle. Be sure to place all the features you noted in step 3.
5. Place the cutout vehicle in its environment with glue or tape. Color the vehicle's environment to complete the activity.

Glossary

allies: countries that are in a helpful association with each other

combat: armed battle

communication: the sending and receiving of information

drag: the slowing force exerted on a moving body by air or water

fleet: a number of ships operating under one command

front lines: the military units closest to the enemy

hatch: an opening

imagination: the ability to form new creative ideas or images

lift: a type of force acting on a wing

periscope: a tube-like instrument that allows people to view objects that are not in the direct line of vision

quarters: where soldiers sleep

radar: the use of radio waves to locate objects

surveillance: close observation of a person or group of people

terrain: the surface features of an area of land

thrust: a force that produces motion

torque: a turning or twisting force

trench warfare: a type of combat in which soldiers fight each other from ditches that face each other

Log on to www.av2books.com

AV² by Weigl brings you media enhanced books that support active learning. Go to www.av2books.com, and enter the special code found on page 2 of this book. You will gain access to enriched and enhanced content that supplements and complements this book. Content includes video, audio, weblinks, quizzes, a slide show, and activities.

Audio
Listen to sections of the book read aloud.

Video
Watch informative video clips.

Embedded Weblinks
Gain additional information for research.

Try This!
Complete activities and hands-on experiments.

WHAT'S ONLINE?

Try This!	**Embedded Weblinks**	**Video**	**EXTRA FEATURES**
Complete an interactive drawing tutorial for each of the six military vehicles in the book.	Learn more about each of the six military vehicles in the book.	Watch a video about military vehicles.	**Audio** Listen to sections of the book read aloud.
			Key Words Study vocabulary, and complete a matching word activity.
			Slide Show View images and captions, and prepare a presentation.
			Quizzes Test your knowledge.

AV² was built to bridge the gap between print and digital. We encourage you to tell us what you like and what you want to see in the future.

Sign up to be an AV² Ambassador at www.av2books.com/ambassador.